D1501632

Penelope Sach

✦✦✦✦✦✦

On Tea

a n d

Healthy Living

✦✦✦✦✦✦

Allen & Unwin

This book is a guide to
herbal teas and their
uses. If you wish to use
herbs in the treatment
of illness and disease,
always consult your
health practitioner first.

First published in 1995
Allen & Unwin Pty Ltd
9 Atchison Street,
St Leonards, NSW 2066 Australia

National Library of Australia
Cataloguing-in-Publication entry

Sach, Penelope.
  Penelope Sach on tea

  ISBN 1 86448 001 7.

  1. Herbal teas. 2. Herbal teas –
  Therapeutic use .I. Title.

641.357

Set in 10/15 pt Weiss
Printed by McPherson's Printing Group, Maryborough
Design by Deborah Brash/Brash Design Pty Ltd
Herb illustrations by Nicola Oram
Additional illustrations by Adrian An (p. 7),
Faye Wilson (p. 24), Roman Stolz (p. 51),
Jimmy Chan (p. 52)

CONTENTS

I dedicate this book to Chloe, Oscar and Miles.
They hold the knowledge of yesterday with
the hope of tomorrow for a society that can be free
of pain and suffering, and a planet that
can be saved in its purity and original beauty.

Penelope Sach

INTRODUCTION

*A*s the clock winds towards the year 2000, our hectic lifestyles and the pressures of everyday living are becoming increasingly demanding. The media inundates us with reports about the state of our health that are both negative and positive, and we are told that major diseases such as heart attacks and cancer are on the rise.

We look for remedies for these disorders and many more in the choices of pharmaceutical drugs, preventative medicines, better lifestyles and even extended vacations. However, these possible solutions can be confusing and debatable and often it becomes just too difficult even to begin to contemplate the best option.

My philosophy is that the simplest things in life are not only the easiest to pursue and generally the most enjoyable, but also the ones that usually work extremely well.

In this book I want to explain *one* simple way that you can improve your health; that you can use immediately without fuss or bother; and that will give positive short-term then long-term results which you will be able to see and feel within yourself. This method, which costs little, takes only a short time to prepare, and has the most important impact on our general health and well-being, is to *drink good quality fluids – regularly*.

Drinks such as herbal teas, filtered water and juices taken throughout the day will give you greater energy and vitality. They will not only flush out unwanted poisons and toxins but will assist to rehydrate all the organs in your body. You will quickly see an improvement in the condition of your skin as it absorbs the fluid and becomes rejuvenated. In addition, your blood will circulate at a better rate; oxygen will be used more efficiently in the body; the kidneys and liver will enjoy the benefits of the increased fluid intake; and you will experience greater well-being. As your health improves you will be better equipped to cope with the pace of our busy lives in the 1990s.

❖

•Internal health is the key to good looks and optimum performance. Like any piece of fine machinery your body will function much more efficiently with quality fluid intake .•

PENELOPE SACH

❖

Herbal teas are a refreshing and delicious way for you to drink more each day. To fully experience the flavour of these teas choose loose-leaf, organically grown herbs. Instead of a dusty tea bag, which after a while can become stale and bland, use a teapot or plunger to make a stimulating or relaxing drink. Also, we can enjoy a drink of blended herbs that tastes quite different from a single-herb tea and offers increased benefits for our health in the long term.

We are now able to combine the centuries-old tradition of using herbs as remedies with modern, scientific research into herbal plants. This will lead to exciting results in the field of preventative medicine and I am sure that we will see herbs and herbal teas becoming even more popular.

Introducing drinks into our diet that do not have high amounts of refined sugar, additives, chemicals and preservatives may seem difficult. Finding filtered water can also be hard at times. We are not going to be perfect in our habits but I hope this book will inspire you to be aware of what you are drinking. It offers some simple guidelines that will assist you either to modify or decrease your intake of certain beverages while increasing your daily dosage of healthy drinks.

I believe that one way to achieve good health is to develop a sound and balanced approach to our diet. You certainly don't have to give up coffee, tea or alcohol completely, provided that you drink these in moderation and that you do not have major health problems. At the same time, you should make a habit of regularly drinking healthy beverages to counteract the effects of these 'baddies'.

Most importantly, whenever we correct a bad habit we need to understand why we are doing this. It should not seem like a chore but a change that we can come to enjoy.

Life can be stressful but I believe a key to overcoming this is to keep things easy and light and not too serious. Enjoy drinking whatever you like but also enjoy drinking to good health.

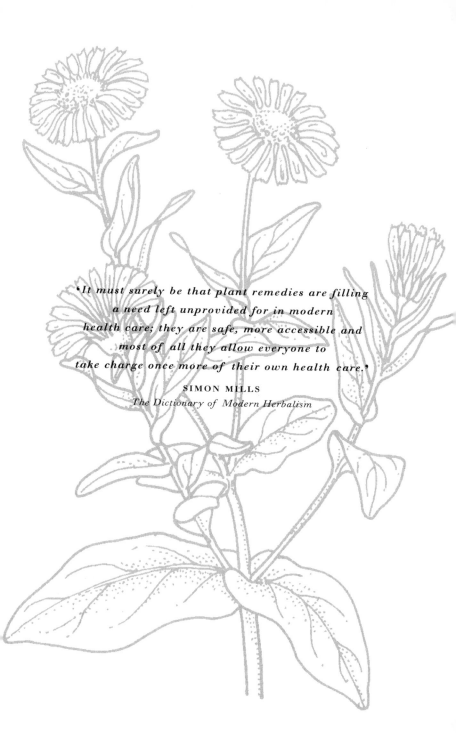

'It must surely be that plant remedies are filling
a need left unprovided for in modern
health care; they are safe, more accessible and
most of all they allow everyone to
take charge once more of their own health care.'

SIMON MILLS
The Dictionary of Modern Herbalism

DRINKING
TO
GOOD HEALTH

*A*FTER oxygen, water is the most important element needed to keep us alive, yet many people do not realise the advantages of drinking water every day. On average, depending on your age, height and weight, it is wise for an adult to drink approximately one to two litres of quality fluid daily, and a child should drink around half a litre, to keep the body healthy.

You may not think that you are dehydrated but it can often be detected by examining the health of the organs in your body. In my clinical experience over the years, I have examined the eyes of many clients with a technique called iridology. By reading the iris, the natural health practitioner is able to see the state of each organ in the body.

Often when I have looked at an iris I have seen a murky brown colour around that area in the eye. This indicates a stagnant bowel and poor circulation. It reminds me of a pond where the water has been stagnating for days. As children, we learned never to drink from still ponds but to find fresh, running water where there is less chance of a build-up of harmful wastes.

Just as water must flow freely to be clean, so must our blood circulate easily though our bodies with a healthy heart as a pump. To help achieve this we have to flush out our systems with a good supply of fresh, clean water and quality liquids every day.

Recently, I treated a client who came to see me because of his weight problem and his lack of energy. He was in his late thirties and led a very hectic life. I did not want to overwhelm him with an involved diet, nor did I suggest a rigid exercise program that I felt he probably would not have time to follow.

Instead, I asked him to drink two glasses of warm, boiled water or herb tea in the morning, with a touch of honey or lemon in it if he wished. I also asked him to repeat this every three hours, for the next ten days. I allowed him two alcoholic drinks, one coffee and one black tea per day.

In that time he not only lost two kilograms but also passed a number of kidney stones, felt much better, and his self-esteem improved. He was happy to continue this regimen and was receptive to making other changes in his diet that I introduced slowly as his workload decreased.

❖

'Water is a perfect eliminator...dissolves all poisonous waste materials and foreign elements in the blood, thereby aiding their elimination .'

JETHRO KLOSS
Back to Eden

❖

We know how important it is to drink copious amounts of water after an alcoholic night out. Usually we are reminded by a headache and a sickly feeling that we must flush out the overdose of alcohol in our bloodstream.

Let's take another simple complaint: aching muscles

after exercise. During exercise muscle tissue contracts and relaxes, and lactic acid is produced as a by product. An accumulation of this acid causes the muscle to ache. By increasing our fluid intake we hydrate the cells and this assists our systems in expelling the lactic acid from the muscles, consequently our bodies recover more quickly.

Also during heavy exercise, our bodies will lose one to two litres of fluid per hour. So remember to replace this fluid in order to avoid dehydration. Drink filtered water before, during and after exercising, perhaps with a sports powder with added magnesium. Heavily sweetened drinks are not absorbed as well or as quickly as plain water so you should avoid them.

You may quickly become bored with plain water so try herbal tea instead. Choose a herb whose taste you enjoy. Also make your selection according to how you feel, for example, peppermint tea will give you a lift, it is deliciously refreshing and it can assist the clearing of the chest and nasal passages. Each herb will give you something different and a combination of herbs will offer another range of flavours and benefits to your health.

Calendula officinalis (Marigold) has been used for centuries for its wound-healing properties.

When you begin to increase your intake of water, urination will become more frequent for the first few days, but with good nutrition and moderate amounts of other quality fluids, the system will stabilise and you will enjoy a clearer bloodstream and hence greater well-being. If you find that you are urinating often over a prolonged time you may need to seek the advice of your health practitioner.

Sometimes you might feel bloated after drinking. This can happen when you have a drink straight after a meal, which slows down the digestive processes. Also, after intense exercise you may feel bloated and experience muscle fatigue, so it may be necessary to replace your electrolytes by adding mainly magnesium and potassium to water. If you drink too much in one go, rather than small amounts frequently, you will experience discomfort and pressure on the stomach muscles and bowel.

Water on its own or in herbal teas is the easiest way to increase your fluid intake. However, if you live in a city or town and do not have access to rainwater, it is important to filter the water you use for drinking and cooking. There are many water filters on the market and I suggest you decide what your needs and budget are then look at the various filters that are available.

A CHOICE OF INFUSIONS

Herbal Teas

◆ HERBAL teas are made from the flowers, leaves, roots, berries and seeds of edible plants. For a refreshing and healthy drink, make a herbal infusion. Do not add milk to this tea but you can stir in some honey or lemon. For medicinal purposes, a herbalist will boil the various parts of the plant, including the roots and the stems, to make a decoction.

Herbal teas do not contain any caffeine (one exception to that rule is the herb kola). Tannin is generally very low in the most common herbal teas, although it can be quite high in some medicinal plants that are used for their astringent effect, such as witch hazel, red raspberry leaves and oak bark. These are used externally for varicose veins and can be drunk in moderate amounts to treat certain ailments.

Fruit Teas

◆ THESE teas are made from fruits and berries in much the same way as herbal tea. They are generally combined for flavour and are very sweet and fruity, consisting of plants such as hibiscus, rose hips, blackberries and dried fruits. Drink them without milk. Fruit teas contain no caffeine and can be drunk anytime as a refreshing infusion. However, people with diabetes should avoid these teas as they have a high sugar content.

Black Tea

❖   BLACK tea comes from the plant *Camellia sinensis*. It contains both caffeine and tannin and can be mixed with milk, sugar or honey.

This is the world's most popular beverage. It was first cultivated in China and then Japan, and in the seventeenth century its cultivation spread to India and Sri Lanka. Today it also grows in Africa and South America.

Camellia sinensis, or *Thea sinensis* as it was formerly known, is an evergreen plant that can grow to 14 metres but the bushes are usually kept to one metre high. The quality and the name of the various types of black tea are determined by the climate and the location where the plants grow, and the method used for hand picking the leaves.

This tea can be divided into *black, oolong* or *green tea*, depending on its fermentation process. Simply put, green tea is not fermented, oolong tea is only given a short fermentation time and black tea is well fermented. Because of the fermentation, or lack of it, during the production of the teas, the three flavours are quite different.

Some of the varieties of black tea include Assam, Darjeeling and Pekoe. Darjeeling is grown widely in India and is one of the few black teas that is not blended. This puts it amongst India's most expensive teas.

Black tea is used for treating highly acidic stomachs due to its tannin content.

GREEN TEA

THIS tea is produced almost exclusively in Japan and China. The varieties are classed as the 'white wines' of Japan with their range of light, delicate flavours. The leaves are graded by age, the youngest being the best. Although green tea has a high caffeine content it is also very rich in vitamin C so it can be drunk to promote good health. Do not add milk or sugar to this tea.

OOLONG TEA

MAINLY produced in Taiwan, oolong is referred to as the 'champagne' of teas. The varieties are deliciously pungent with a fruity flavour. Ti Kuan Yin is particularly popular. Orange pekoe is a scented oolong that is mixed with gardenia or jasmine flowers.

Flavoured Black Teas

❖ FLAVOURED or scented black teas are often confused with herbal teas. In fact, they are black teas that have been combined with a flavour or essence which the tea-leaves absorb. For example, vanilla, mango and peach teas are black teas with an added essence. Sometimes pieces of the dried fruit, such as mango, may be scattered throughout the tea but this is for appearance only as the pieces do not give the flavour. This is achieved when the essence of mango is absorbed into the leaves.

These teas contain both caffeine and tannin. You can drink them with milk and sugar.

A HISTORY
OF
HERBS AND TEAS

$\mathcal{T}$HE history of tea can be traced back to China in 2730 BC and to the Emperor Shen Nung, who was highly respected for his botanical knowledge. He studied the uses of plants such as opium poppies, hemp, aconite and rhubarb, and also discovered that a brew could be made from the leaves of *Camellia sinensis* or *Thea sinensis*. This is the plant we still use today for black tea.

Shen Nung observed that people who boiled their drinking water were healthier than those who drank the impurities in unboiled water, so he took up this practice himself. It is believed that while the Emperor was boiling some water, leaves from the *Camellia sinensis* plant fell into his pot. He drank this brew and found it to be refreshing and flavoursome. This is one explanation for the origins of black tea.

The Indians have their own legends about tea drinking. A patriarch named Darma, who devoted seven years of sleepless contemplation to reaching the perfection of Buddha, began to feel sleepy during his fifth year. As he was fighting against the weakness of the flesh he was inspired to pick some leaves from the *Camellia sinensis* plant and chew them. This restored his control over his mind, body and spirit so that he could meditate for a further two years.

A Japanese hermit was attempting to overcome a similar weariness when, it is said, he cut off his eyelashes in a fit of frustration and threw them on the ground. They took root and grew as tea plants.

In these stories the wise men were rewarded with the stimulant in black tea that we know as caffeine. To quote Shen Nung:

Tea is better than wine for it leadeth not to intoxication, neither does it cause a man to say foolish things and repent thereof in his sober moments. It is better than water for it does not carry disease, neither does it act like poison as water does when the wells contain foul and rotten matter.

By the fifth century, tea had become popular and was traded between countries. However, it was not until the eighth century that a Chinese Buddhist priest, Lu Yu, refined the way tea should be manufactured. He also raised the act of tea drinking to a spiritual level. Interestingly, Lu Yu's principles of manufacturing and preparing black tea are still used today, and he is respected by tea merchants as their patron.

❖

'Tea tempers the spirit, harmonises the mind, dispels lassitude and relieves fatigue, awakens the thought and prevents drowsiness.'

LU YU
The Classic Art of Tea

❖

The ritual of tea drinking established by Lu Yu suited the Confucian way of life in China. It symbolised temperance, moderation and calmness. Tea became more than a national drink in that country. It was a part of the religion, an essential aspect of one's daily routine, comforting, reassuring and also, delicious to drink. Tea also became a subject of poetry in China.

The first cup moistens my lips and throat
the second cup breaks my loneliness
the third cup searches my barren entrail
but to find therein some five thousand volumes of ideographs;
The fourth cup raises a slight perspiration –
all the wrongs of life pour out through my pores,
At the fifth cup I am purified,
The sixth cup calls me to the realms of the immortals
The seventh cup – ah but I could take no more
I only feel the breath of the cool breeze that passes
    on my sleeves.

It is believed that tea was brought to England many decades after this, in the sixteenth century during the reign of Queen Elizabeth I. Before the introduction of tea to her country, the Queen was said to have breakfasted on 'bread, flesh and a gallon of beer'!

Queen Elizabeth I established a trade route between China and England to import tea. The first fleet of trading vessels was sent in 1556 under Sir Robert Dudley, but nothing was ever heard of them again. In 1600, the East India Company was established, and traded between the Cape of Good Hope and the Strait of Magellan. Tea became fashionable throughout England and in 1660 Charles II imposed the first English tea taxes. By 1725, England had imported a total of 250,000 pounds of tea. Eight years later, its imports averaged 24,000,000 pounds per year.

The English poet William Cowper wrote:

Now stir the fire, and close the shutters fast,
Let fall the curtains, wheel the sofa round
And while the bubbling and loud hissing urn
throws up a steamy column,
the cups that cheer but not inebriate wait on each,
So let us welcome peaceful evening in.

Between the 1840s and 1870s, the famous 'tea clippers' sailed from North America and England to Canton in China to pick up precious cargoes of tea to take back to the West.

❖

Herbal teas hold a fascinating and important place in both medical and culinary history and there are many references to their uses that have been passed down through the centuries. Since the time of the Greek and Roman empires, and perhaps before, plants have been used in worship; to drink or smoke; to decorate the living body; and to embalm it in preparation for the afterlife.

❖

•Like the great medicinal traditions of Ancient China,
India and Egypt, Hippocrates' medicine had
stressed the idea of balance — mental, emotional
and physical — as essential to health;
disease was a disturbance of this balance.•

JETHRO KLOSS
Back to Eden

❖

In 460 BC, the most famous physician of ancient Greece, Hippocrates, began to create an order to describe the various properties of plants and he recorded in detail their pharmacological actions. Hippocrates wrote: 'Let food be your medicine and medicine be your food'.

Following Hippocrates, the Roman naturalist Pliny the Elder, born in Verona in 23 AD, spent his life recording the botanical and medicinal details of hundreds of plants; undertaking his own research and drawing on the information collected by others. His work on herbs and other plants amounted to 37 books.

Galen, born in Pergamos in Asia Minor, was the most famous and most respected of physicians after Hippocrates. In his works he refers to numerous herbal remedies for the treatment of disease, including the use of mineral substances upon which our allopathic and homoeopathic systems of medicine are based.

When the Roman Empire disintegrated, the study of medicine fell out of favour. Herbal plants, remedies and mixtures began to be associated with superstitions and many strange stories were spread about them. Because women had become accomplished herbalists, treating their families and local communities, many were singled out as having special abilities. These abilities were often misunderstood and came to be regarded as witchcraft, and the plants and their powers were perceived as belonging to the realm of magic. Many of the so-called witches, who were killed for their healing abilities, were only using the powerful therapeutic substances of the plants. Just as in any other time up to the present, some of the women were charlatans but others were highly skilled and principled healers.

In the Middle Ages, when women were being burnt at

the stake, much of the knowledge about healing was lost. Instead, Christians looked upon disease as a punishment from God, which could only be cured by repentance and prayer. It was not until medical schools were established in Europe that people began to realise they needed treatment apart from praying to an appropriate saint.

❖

❦Botany and medicine came down the ages hand in hand until the seventeenth century, then both arts became scientific, their ways parted...the botanical books ignored the medicinal properties of plants and the medical books contained no plant lore.❦

HILDA LEYEL

A History of Herbal Plants, by Richard le Strange

❖

While Europe was in the midst of the Reformation, the great English herbalist Nicholas Culpeper was writing on the use of plants in relation to his medical practice. His book, *The English Physician*, published in 1653 is still used today for the important information it offers about plants.

At this time, Europeans were settling in North America and much of Culpeper's advice on plants, their growing time and medicinal effects, was used by those early settlers. Housewives began to pick the native plants of North America to enrich their diet. Certain berries and herbs became popular for treating the sick. For example, lobelia, capsicum and fringetree – which are still used widely today – were used to cure all sorts of ailments. They were made into teas and tinctures to use both internally and to be applied externally.

Children were relieved of fevers by drinking elder flower tea. Joint pain and gout were treated with tea made from nettles, and kidney stones could be passed with the help of a brew of barley water, cornsilk and buchu. Sufferers of digestive disorders were given chamomile tea to soothe and relax muscle spasms, while babies were given it when they were teething. Dandelion roots were collected and brewed for headaches, and peppermint and spearmint teas were drunk to assist in treating bile, liver and mucous problems, to relieve coughs and spasms and to calm an agitated system.

The art of preparing herbal tea to treat various ailments was handed down from generation to generation. Then, whether correctly or incorrectly, certain teas became an essential part of one's health care. Much of the knowledge of plants was trial and error as there was certainly no way to test their properties scientifically. Instead, careful observation of the plants taught the herbalist to recognise distinct changes in odours or colours that could indicate that the plant would be fatal when ingested, or that it could be beneficial for treating certain ailments. The herbalist also took into account the seasons and the phases of the moon, as these would affect the herbs.

Up until World War II, many families in Europe, North America and Asia were using plants from the fields to cure their ailments and to increase their well-being and vitality. One of the greatest herbs, *Calendula officinalis*, or marigold, was widely used during the war as an antiseptic in English hospitals and in treating soldiers' cuts and wounds on the battlefield.

During the years between 1945 and the 1960s, herbal medicine took a back seat. The discovery of penicillin and its use in treating infectious disease, which became fully realised in the 1940s, and the development of the oral contraceptive pill in the 1960s, were the highlights of the medical revolution. The use of plants to treat ill-health was looked upon as 'hippy', 'alternative' and non-scientific. Even though there was such a long tradition of using herbs as remedies and as teas, all medicinal treatments during this time had to be scientifically proven, otherwise they were regarded as quaint but useless folklore.

Like many things in history, however, the attitudes towards herbal teas and medicine have taken a complete turn about. In the 1990s we are taking a completely new look at an ancient form of medicine. Pharmaceutical companies are now spending millions of dollars to research plants and their medicinal effects. This information should be of enormous benefit to our health in the future.

Today we recognise the importance of good eating and drinking in preventative health care. We are open to combining the traditional knowledge of herbs with the scientific findings into their many uses. We realise that herbal teas can be just as useful now as they were in the Middle Ages. However, in the 1990s we use them in conjunction with our modern medical knowledge. They help our bodies to flush out the residue from drug medication, caffeine, pollutants, bowel toxicity and poor diet. Herbal teas also help to relieve the anxiety and stress that are so much a part of our lives as we rush towards 2000.

HERBAL TEA
FOR PLEASURE AND
HEALTH

'Love and scandal are the best sweeteners of tea.'
HENRY FIELDING

❖

THE variety of herbs is so vast that you can select a tea to suit your individual taste. Then, depending on which herb or mixture of herbs you choose, they can have a mild effect on stimulating the kidneys, calming the digestive system, aiding circulation and most importantly, they will put water back into your body.

In addition to improving our immediate well-being, herbal teas help us to improve our health over the long term. This is further enhanced when a herbalist blends two or more herbs to draw on the therapeutic effects of each plant. This also creates different flavours and gives you an even wider selection of teas from which to choose.

Generally the herbal teas that we most enjoy are the ones that our bodies need. For example, people who are stressed often crave chamomile. If you have a cold, there is nothing better than a pot of peppermint tea with honey and lemon to soothe the throat and help to clear the sinus passages.

Once you have found your favourite range of herbs, you will discover how herbal teas can soften plain water, making it easier and more enjoyable to drink regularly.

Selecting the best herbal tea to help you to maintain or improve your own well-being can become confusing. However, the rules are simple. At first select the herb whose taste you enjoy, follow the guidelines given in this chapter and consult a herbalist about specific ailments.

Selecting Herbs

❖ PLANTS can be divided into groups that are related to different systems in the body. We can choose a herb from one group or select herbs from three or four groups and drink this mixture regularly.

Chinese herbalists often use several dried herbs blended together. They boil the mixture for up to twenty minutes and prescribe it to be drunk three times a day. During the boiling, the active ingredients in the plants are released into the water in a concentrated form. Through this the herbalist produces a therapeutic mixture that will treat the illness more quickly than a weaker infusion of the same ingredients.

Most people do not have time to prepare this strength of decoction regularly, so a concentrate, which has already been boiled or soaked in distilled water and preserved in a small amount of medicinal alcohol, is prescribed. Generally one teaspoon must be taken instead of one cup of the weaker tea, three times a day. This needs to be diluted as the water helps to carry the medicine to the specific organs.

Herbal teas will always be beneficial to your health, but if you have a specific problem you should select a herb that is known to help rectify that ailment. If it is a serious illness or disease you should seek medical advice and ask your herbalist to prescribe a complementary course of herbs that you can safely take in conjunction with the medical treatment.

Herbs for Stress-related Illness

❖ THE herbs in this group are referred to as nervines, antispasmodics or relaxants. They are used to assist in treating such disorders as nervous fatigue, exhaustion and mental depression.

Like every other part of our body, the nerve tissues need to be nourished and nurtured and when they are overworked they will become exhausted. To treat a tired and strained nervous system you can drink teas made from chamomile, lavender, rosemary and vervain. Less common herbs that will also be effective are St John's wort, damiara, skullcap, oats and ginseng.

Herbs for Digestive, Bowel and Liver Disorders

❖ THESE herbs can aid the breakdown of food and its elimination. They help to stimulate enzyme reactions; to absorb wind and flatulence; assist the clearing of the bowel; and they relax the muscles of the stomach and bowel when stress causes your stomach to become tight.

Many of these herbs taste unpleasant as they contain bitter substances, so often they are used as a concentrate medicine rather than as a tea.

These plants will help to stimulate your digestion, and for this reason they are sometimes included in cooking. They are also ideal for the elderly, who often need help to digest their food; for sufferers of a long illness; and for people who have lost their appetite.

Some of the herbs in this category are angelica, cardamom, celery, cinnamon, ginger, fenugreek, parsley, thyme and peppermint. Other plants used by herbalists are golden seal, dandelion, gentian and barberry.

The bowel often needs soothing herbs, or a herb that has a very gentle laxative action to assist in the elimination of toxins. Herbalists traditionally referred to these herbs as mucilaginous. They contain a sticky substance that expands with water and helps to absorb and remove wastes. Slippery elm bark and marshmallow, for example, can be mixed with water to make a drink that will soothe the stomach, bowel, ulcers and irritability of the digestive system.

Herbs to treat the liver and gall bladder can also fall into the digestive category. In our society, the liver is often overworked with alcohol, rich foods, not enough water, and environmental pollutants. Herbs that

Marshmallow

should be drunk regularly to help the liver and gall bladder are dandelion and chicory as well as the vegetable, artichoke. The less common herbs in this group are St Mary's thistle, fringetree and chelidonium.

Herbs for the Bronchials

❖ FOR centuries, many herbs have been used successfully to treat chronic conditions of the lungs, sinuses and throat. Bronchitis, asthma, tonsillitis and ear infections are some of the problems that still seem to affect most of us sometime in our lives. There are many herbs that can prevent if not cure some of these unpleasant conditions before you need to turn to the stronger pharmaceuticals, which unfortunately have undesirable side effects.

Bronchial herbs can soothe the irritated, inflamed membranes; help you to cough up excess mucus; relax tight bronchial spasms (asthma); and assist in arresting foreign allergens in the upper respiratory organs.

Common herbs in this group are peppermint, ginger, liquorice, horseradish, garlic and cayenne. Other examples that herbalists prescribe as teas and concentrates are mullein, elecampane, thyme and grindelia

Herbs for the Joints

❖ SINCE sport and all forms of exercise have become so important in our preventative health regimes and in increasing our feeling of well-being, the incidence of joint pain, injuries and arthritis seems to be on the rise. Two other conditions related to our skeletal system are gout and rheumatism.

To correct these problems, it is vital to keep your

fluid intake to its maximum so that the joints and muscles are 'bathed' in liquid. Drinking is also important in order to flush out lactic acid and residue from the painful area. In these situations, herbal teas are the ideal way to give your body the fluid it needs.

Nettle tea is the most appropriate tea to treat these problems. It has been used for centuries to treat painful joints. The Roman armies, for example, took it internally and externally before going into battle to stimulate and lubricate their joints.

Drinking nettle tea is an effective way to withdraw lactic acid and uric acid from the body. Knowing this, the medieval kings would drink it after over-indulging themselves with food and alcohol. They also used it as a tea and as a foot bath to relieve the pain of gout.

Other herbs that will help you to maintain healthy joints and to relieve in arthritis are celery seeds, willow bark, bogbean, prickly ash and guaiacum.

Herbs for the Bladder

❖ MANY men, women and even children suffer bladder infections, fluid retention and associated problems. Kidney stones and prostate stones have also become common.

I believe these disorders occur when we do not drink enough fluid to flush the bacteria and wastes out of our bodies. There are also certain herbs that can be used to prevent these disorders.

Old-fashioned barley water (not the sort made commercially) is the most wonderful drink for the prevention of bladder problems and to assist in the elimination of urine. Boil four teaspoons of barley in four cups of water for twenty minutes. Drink this regularly, and add herbs and honey to give it some flavour if you wish. Barley water soothes the inflamed areas with its mucilage effect and mixed with antiseptic teas, such as thyme, and a few drops of tea-tree oil, it will have a profound effect.

Other common teas that can be drunk regularly to keep the bladder clean and healthy are buchu, uva ursi, celery and parsley seeds, juniper and cornsilk.

Herbs for the Skin

❖ EVERYONE wants to have healthy, glowing skin. It is a true reflection of your condition and it will indicate the health of your liver, whether you are suffering from allergies and stress, and if your elimination system is functioning correctly.

Herbalists have traditionally referred to plants used for treating the skin as detoxifying herbs. They act slowly and safely, cleaning out poisons from the blood and purifying the system. These herbs stimulate the white blood cells to enhance our immune systems and help our bodies to fight bacteria without the need for antibiotics.

Common herbs in this group are red clover, echinacaea, burdock, nettle, hypericum and astragalus. They are often mixed with liver and digestive herbs and drunk as a tea.

Herbs for the Heart and Circulation

❖ CARDIOVASCULAR disease is a major killer in Australia. It can be hereditary but other causes include high stress levels, poor diet and smoking.

We should always seek qualified medical treatment for this condition but there are herbs that complement other medication. A doctor should be consulted if you are taking any herbal remedies in addition to medication for heart disease.

Hawthorn berries and rosemary have been used for centuries by herbalists as a tonic for the heart.

Hawthorn berries

Other herbs for sluggish circulation – such as varicose veins, cold hands and feet – are ginger, capsicum and ginkgo. These restore warmth to the extremities of the body and assist in treating tinnitus and brain fatigue.

My Favourite Herbal Teas

❖ MANY people ask me what my favourite herbal teas are. They also want to know which are the most beneficial to our health, can be drunk safely every day and also taste pleasant. On the pages that follow, I have selected eight herbs that I believe you will find delicious to drink as a tea and they will help you to maintain or improve your well-being.

CHAMOMILE

*W*ILD chamomile or german chamomile (*Matricaria recutita*) is the most widely used variety. The plant can grow to 60 centimetres in height and it is characterised by a beautiful yellow flower with a very strong, distinctive aroma.

This plant has been used for centuries for its calming effect on the nerves and stomach, to relieve skin rashes and allergies, and for its assistance in sleeplessness and headaches. Taken internally or externally, chamomile is an excellent and safe herb for everyday use.

The plant contains a volatile oil that includes an active substance, chamazulene, which has been found to have anti-allergic actions. This means that it can safely be used in hair and skin cosmetics and as a wash for stinging, tired eyes. As a mouth wash and a foot bath, chamomile will help to soothe and restore skin tissue. It is also safe as a wash for babies with irritated or inflamed skin. Follow this wash with an application of an ointment made from calendula and chamomile.

Herbalists use chamomile to ease all forms of stomach upsets, whether they are due to poor eating habits, a bad food combination, stomach ulcers, acidity or stress. It has a mild antispasmodic action that assists in calming the tight spasms of the stomach or intestinal wall if you are under stress or experiencing digestive problems. It is believed this action is due to a therapeutic substance called dicyclic ether. Chamomile, used internally or externally, also relieves arthritic inflammation or pain and swelling.

The essential oil in chamomile is widely used in aromatherapy for its anti-inflammatory, calming effect and it is often added to massage oils.

Drink chamomile tea after eating rich foods, to ease the effects of gastritis and food poisoning, and to overcome sleeplessness. Also, give it to babies when they are teething. If you are tense and under pressure, drink the tea throughout the day and at night. If you are not suffering from stress or anxiety, however, you do not need to drink chamomile during the day, and if you do it may actually make you feel sleepy.

PEPPERMINT

*P*EPPERMINT (*Mentha x piperita*) is a hybrid of water-mint and spearmint. The plant has smooth leaves and a purple flower. It is a perennial and is commonly found in Europe but grows well in most countries.

In the seventeenth century, the English herbalist Nicholas Culpeper wrote that peppermint was useful for 'complaints of the stomach'. A pharmacist named Joseph Bosisto brought it to the colony of Australia, so it has been cultivated here for two centuries. Now very high-quality peppermint grows in Victoria and Tasmania.

Its wonderful, strong odour is due to its volatile oils, which include menthol. Because of this oil, peppermint can be used for many different ailments in a variety of forms from tea, to condiments, to inhalants and liniments.

Peppermint was the most widely used herb in ancient Egypt. Dioscorides prescribed the juice of mint with vinegar to stop wounds bleeding, and also to treat swollen, sore gums and children's sores. The leaves were used to whiten teeth and menthol is added to most toothpastes and mouthwashes even today.

We now know that peppermint oil has a relaxing effect on the gall bladder, which allows the bile to flow more easily, thereby assisting indigestion, dyspepsia and 'acid stomach'. Many digestive tablets contain a large component of menthol for this very reason.

Peppermint not only calms the gall bladder but also eases the stomach muscles and bowel, and assists in dispensing flatulence. If you suffer from nausea or travel sickness, inhale the aromas of the oil and drink or inhale peppermint tea. The tea also helps to relieve mucous congestion in the nose and breathing passages, hence peppermint is a primary ingredient in most cough mixtures.

In 1895 in Australia, everyone knew of the famous 'Great Peppermint Cure', now called 'Woods Peppermint Cough Syrup'. By 1901 it had sold one million bottles, and later it became a panacea for the soldiers during the First World War. 'The men preferred it to grog, as it warmed them thoroughly while lying out on the veldt.'

Peppermint can be used in different ways according to the seasons. During the winter months we can drink hot peppermint tea for warmth, to invigorate our cold bodies, to treat colds and the flu, and to ease our stomachs after eating hearty winter meals.

In summer, peppermint tea is a delicious and refreshing drink when served cold. Children can suck on homemade peppermint and honey ice-blocks, free of the chemicals and additives of most ice-creams.

DANDELION

*D*ANDELION (*Taraxacum officinale*) might appear to some to be a common weed. However, it is an extremely versatile herb that is used by both herbalists and gardeners.

Experiments have verified that the dandelion root absorbs three times the amount of iron from the soil than is taken up by any other plant. At the same time, because it works so well as a nitrogen fixer, it enriches the soil wherever it grows, and releases its properties of iron, copper and other nutrients when it decomposes.

The dandelion is particularly important for our cities because Russian studies have found that it readily absorbs metal pollutants from the atmosphere. It can therefore be used in a small way to help control air pollution. In view of this, you should only buy dandelions that are organically grown, otherwise the plant would have absorbed very high levels of pesticides.

Tea can be made from either the leaves or the root of the dandelion. Each part works quite differently on our bodies. Drinking tea made from the root can taste a little bitter, but mixed with milk and honey as a coffee substitute, it tastes quite delicious.

Dandelion root is remarkable for its ability to stimulate the bile and to assist the functioning of the liver and the spleen.

Avicenna, the great Arabian physician of the eleventh century, loved to prescribe it for 'evacuating bile' and 'to gradually restore health'. The roots are great long-term liver detoxifiers and many herbalists use them for treating constipation, sluggish liver and overdoses of alcohol and rich food.

Both the leaves and roots are useful in assisting weight loss as they have a diuretic effect that is beneficial for people who have fluid retention. The leaves are safe to drink as a tea because they do not deplete the body of potassium, and studies undertaken in Romania suggest that the leaf may be one of the most powerful therapeutic agents for both fluid and weight reduction.

Dandelion has been used by the Chinese, in India, and by monks in Nepal for hundreds of years to treat complaints of the liver. Today, research is being carried out on the properties of its active constituents to determine how it assists liver function so well, and to give a scientific explanation for something that herbalists have known about for centuries.

LIQUORICE

THROUGHOUT history, liquorice (*Glycyrrhiza glabra*) has been used to treat coughs, stomach problems and as confectionery. I am not referring here to the commercial sweets called liquorice that are sold today. In fact, most of these sweets contain no liquorice but are flavoured with aniseed oil. Pure liquorice root is sweet because it contains a saponin called glycyrrhizic acid, which is about fifty times sweeter than sugar.

The Greek physician Theophrastus prescribed liquorice for quenching thirst and for cramps caused by stomach ulcers and asthma. Napoleon would always chew on a piece of liquorice root.

In 1940, a Dutch doctor named Rovers noted that patients were being cured of peptic ulcers by high doses of liquorice extract. However, on these doses they also suffered fluid retention and raised blood pressure. Later, in the 1950s, Dutch researchers found that liquorice extract had a dramatic effect in maintaining electrolyte equilibrium in patients with Addison's Disease. This disease is due to adrenal cortex malfunction and cortisone is generally prescribed to treat it. By using liquorice, which helps the adrenal cortex to produce its own cortico-steroids together with cortisone, excellent results were achieved. Liquorice was then used as a crude ointment that had a cortisone-like action and it assisted in curing chronic eczema.

If you take liquorice as a concentrated extract your health should be monitored by a herbalist or doctor if you suffer from kidney problems, fluid retention or cardiovascular problems. The tea can be safely drunk after or between meals, three to four times a day to assist in relieving stomach acid, effects from stomach ulcers and also irritating bronchial conditions. In fact, Pliny discovered that liquorice was a good remedy for both stomach and mouth ulcers.

I find that it is a wonderful preventative herb. Liquorice is also a successful restorer in stressful conditions due to its tonic effect, particularly on the exhausted adrenal glands. It is interesting to note that athletes often crave this herb.

NETTLE

*M*ANY people know the stinging nettle (*Urtica dioica*) for its unpleasant feel against the skin. In ancient times however, it was eaten as a steamed green vegetable, high in vitamins A and C. Today herbalists find it invaluable for treating many diseases.

The most effective way to consume nettles is as a tea, although the taste is quite bland. So I suggest that you mix it with chamomile or peppermint to improve the flavour. Nettle tea can be marvellous as a wash for children with allergic eczema when it is combined with the anti-allergic, anti-inflammatory effects of chamomile. Children can also sip half a cup of this tea with honey two to three times a day.

You can drink two to three cups of nettle tea daily for the treatment of rheumatism, gout and skin irritations such as eczema and dermatitis, as well as bleeding noses and haemorrhoids.

With changes occurring in our diet, many children and teenagers can become anaemic. Eliminating red meat has been a trend for the last decade, but the iron-rich protein is not always substituted with other rich sources of iron like greens, grains, soya products and berries. For the tired, allergic and anaemic child or teenager this herb is extremely useful. Nettle tea also assists the production of milk in humans and animals because of its nutritive properties and high iron content.

The old herbalists always used this herb in their formulas for adult onset diabetes, but even today we do not understand exactly how nettles assist this condition. Although not enough scientific research has been done on this plant as yet, we do know that it has no side effects.

Nettles have a variety of uses. Thread was spun from this herb in Scandinavia, and even up to the middle of this century fibre spun from nettles was manufactured in Scotland. Beer was made from nettles which are also an excellent food for animals. The seeds of nettles mixed with the food for poultry increases the hens' laying power.

Nettle is often used in hair tonics and the ancient herbalists believed that this herb was effective in stopping hair loss. This may be because of its high nutritive effect but as yet we do not know this for sure.

In my clinical experience I have found this herb to be effective in treating a wide range of illnesses including gout and rheumatism associated with allergies. Ask your herbalist to recommend appropriate doses and try it before resorting to the stronger pharmaceutical drugs.

ELM BARK

*'And the fruit thereof shall be for
meat and the leaf thereof for medicine.'*

EZEKIEL, 47:12

❖

SLIPPERY ELM BARK (*Ulmus fulva*), also referred to as
red elm, is an extremely versatile herb and nutrient.
If I could use only one herb to treat numerous ailments
experienced by men, women and children in this hectic
age it would be elm bark.

This powder is obtained from the inner bark of a tree
which commonly grows in eastern and central North
America. Its chemical composition is uncomplicated.
Elm bark consists of mucilage (a thick paste-like substance), with a small amount of tannin and starch. It is
the mucilage that is marvellous for treating inflamed
membranes. Internally this includes peptic ulcers, acid
stomachs, irritable bowel, diverticulitis, diarrhoea,
dysentery and sore throats. Externally it includes burns,
ulcers and wounds.

The mucilage is taken up by water, hence it is ideal to
use as a tea. Depending on the amount used, the drink
becomes a little thick and this lines and 'poultices' the
inflamed areas of the body. The tea soothes the areas
and prevents foreign substances from being absorbed
into the painful areas, such as peptic and duodenal
ulcers. Therefore, it should be drunk before eating.

Mixed with chamomile, elm bark tea is a perfect way to calm the 'nervous acid' feeling that you get in your stomach during periods of high stress. This same tea is excellent for those recovering from a long illness, or for anyone who does not eat enough during the day.

It is safe for the very young and very old. In fact, a tablespoon of the powder boiled in a pint of milk is a nourishing food for a baby being weaned. It will prevent bowel complications and will give the baby a healthy start in life.

Many famous rock stars and opera singers drink elm bark tea before, during and after their performance, to soothe and relax their throats. If you are suffering from a cold or the flu, mix the powder with peppermint or chamomile tea. Children don't mind the taste of this tea if they have tonsillitis or lose their voice.

A multivitamin tablet taken with this tea and a piece of fruit is a nutritious snack. I have also found elm bark to be of great benefit to those who don't eat breakfast. One to two teaspoons of the powder mixed with milk or water lines the stomach and leads to better nutrition. Also, it is a good way to line the stomach before drinking alcohol. Then after drinking alcohol or eating rich foods drink elm bark tea to assist the dilution of acid in the stomach.

It is the most beneficial tea, so include it in you diet every day.

GINSENG

*G*INSENG is a wonderful herb for treating exhaustion and stress. There are three varieties: Siberian ginseng (*Eleutherococcus senticosus*); Chinese ginseng (*Panax ginseng*); and the botanically unrelated Indian ginseng (*Withania somnifera*). Each has the ability to improve your general state of health, to increase your energy levels and your resistance to disease.

Siberian ginseng will increase your capacity to withstand adverse environmental and working conditions. Sailors, rescue workers, truck drivers, pilots and astronauts have used it to improve their stamina. In tests it was found that people taking ginseng or drinking it as a tea increased their mental and physical output.

In Russia, this herb is used by Olympic athletes to increase their capacity for endurance and concentration. As it has only a mild stimulant and anabolic effect its use is not prohibited during competitive sport. When given to patients with cancer, Siberian ginseng has minimised the side effects of chemotherapy and surgery, hastened the healing process, and increased the patient's well-being. Short courses of ginseng are also beneficial for children with dysentery.

The studies on the uses of Siberian ginseng have recorded a general absence of side effects. However because of its strength as a stimulant, I would advise you to use it moderately if you suffer insomnia, heart palpitation or high blood pressure. A herbalist will recommend a course for six weeks with a two-week break, but continuous use if you are suffering a long-term illness.

Chinese ginseng is believed to assist the body in combating stress by improving the ability of the adrenal cortex to deal with it. Tea made from it can be used to improve concentration, increase stamina, for stress resistance, and to enhance your physical condition if you are training for a sports competition. Remember, however, that you should speak to your herbalist about the correct dosage for your needs.

Indian ginseng calms the over-sensitive person who does not need to be 'hyped up' by the other two varieties. It will help an anxious person to cope with stressful situations. Also, it helps to conserve energy, feed the adrenal glands in a gentle way and is a great asset to people suffering long-term stress and exhaustion. It can be used over a long time without causing harmful side effects.

I believe that ginseng will help you to cope with stress and greatly improve your well-being. Speak to your herbalist about the many benefits of this herb and they can assist you in selecting the correct variety of ginseng and the appropriate dosage for your needs.

HAWTHORN

Crataegus monogyna has been associated with the heart for hundreds of years. Now, through scientific studies, it is known to have a considerable role to play in caring for the health of the cardiovascular system. Through this research it was found that prescribed doses of hawthorn would assist arterial blood pressure, reduce the heart rate and allow a better uptake of oxygen.

It is generally the berries from the hawthorn plant that are used to make tea but the leaves and flowers can be added. Often when making herbal medicine a mixture of both is used.

Hawthorn has an extremely interesting history. In 1534, an expedition in Canada led by Jacques Cartier was afflicted with scurvy. The Indians told the explorers to drink a boiled decoction of the berries and to use it externally as a poultice on their wounds. By following this advice the men recovered.

The ancient herbalists believed that hawthorn would normalise the action of the heart in a gentle way, whether it needed depressing or stimulating. I find that people who suffer sluggish circulation, varicose veins and panic attacks often love to drink this herb as a tea or to take it in more concentrated forms.

THE ART OF
BREWING
HERBAL TEA

*T*EA can be prepared in different ways depending on whether you want a refreshing drink or to use it as a medication. Throughout history, such factors as culture and religion have determined how various teas are selected and prepared. Today we have to blend the art of making tea with our hectic lifestyles.

The loose leaves, flowers or berries of the herb always give the best results. You will never obtain the fullness of flavour, the richness of the herb and its potential benefits with a tea bag. The paper constricts the flow of the flavours and the leaves in a tea bag have been powdered, losing much of their therapeutic properties, especially their essential oils.

Fresh leaves from herbs such as peppermint, chamomile, lemongrass and sage, can be used straight from the garden. Remember though, that these leaves must be bruised to release their oils then the flavour will be extracted by the boiling water.

Always try to use good quality, organic herbs for your tea. Then treat this tea in the same way as fresh food while in storage. Keep it cool, preferably below 14 degrees, and in hot, humid climates store the tea-leaves in the refrigerator.

It is always best to use filtered water to make tea as this will protect you from the chemicals and pollutants that can be in our tap water. At the same time you receive the benefits that pure water bring. Boiling unfiltered water will not guarantee the removal of chemicals. In fact, John D. Kirschmann in his book *Nutrition Almanac*, writes that:

> *Boiling water, whether hot or cold tap water or bottled water, for long periods of time for purification is not recommended because although the bacteria will be destroyed, the purest water will be lost in the form of steam and any heavy metals or nitrates in the water will be more concentrated.*

Boil water in glass or stainless steel, not aluminium. When making Chinese tea the water is often not brought to its full boiling point. With herb tea, however, it is appropriate to bring the water to full boil and pour it immediately over the herbs.

Glass teapots show the beauty of the herbs, particularly when flowers and buds are included in the tea. Also, glass retains the heat well and won't taint the flavour. Herb tea can be made in a porcelain teapot if you do not have a glass plunger or pot. No matter what the teapot is made of, it should be kept for herbal teas only. Always make black teas or coffee in a different pot so that the herbs do not take on the taste of these other drinks.

Remember to avoid using strong detergents when cleaning the inside of the teapot; rinse it with water instead. Once every one to two months you will need to wash your glass teapot to remove the stains that build up from the herbs. Use a mild detergent then rinse the pot thoroughly in clean water.

When using a glass teapot it is not necessary to warm it first. This is only important for pots made of porcelain or thicker pottery that are usually cool and would otherwise quickly lose the heat of the tea.

After pouring over the boiling water, herbal tea made from leaves and flowers should stand for approximately three to four minutes, and up to fifteen minutes if it contains berries and roots. This additional time is necessary because the boiling water seeps into the harder parts of the herb more slowly, gradually penetrating the fibres and extracting the plant's flavours and medicinal substances.

As with any tea, some people may prefer a weaker flavour so use less herbs and let it stand for a shorter time. Of course, do the reverse for a stronger tea.

Dried loose herbs can be topped up with more boiling water and used three or four times without losing all their flavour. As the taste of herbs is often quite strong, the freshly boiled water will continue to bring out the flavour and the beneficial elements in the tea.

You can add honey or lemon to herbal teas but generally they are delicious as they are. If you have a sweet tooth choose a naturally sweet herb tea, such as liquorice, or a fruit tea that will not need any additional sweeteners. These teas are particularly

Blackberry

beneficial for hyperactive children and for people suffering from anxiety or stress.

It is always a joy to experience the social act of tea drinking, whether it be in a formal setting in Japan, the afternoon tea gathering in Britain, the pleasure of a herbal tea at a hotel amongst business associates and colleagues, or on a verandah with friends. You can even enjoy taking time out during a hectic day to have a cup of tea on your own and relax a little.

The Tea Ceremony

❖ THE Japanese people have taken the ritual of tea drinking and made it into a refined and beautiful ceremony. To this day, the tea ceremony is practised as a reminder of the spiritual world that exists within each of us.

Here are the five principles of the Japanese tea ceremony. I believe that we can all gain something from them.

Hygiene: as a form of respect of doing things well

Harmony: between all those participating in the ceremony

Humility: a low doorway to enter; teaches the evils of egotism

Reverence: for each other and the tea, and its implements

Peace: the self-discipline not to say any word which will offend.

DAILY
DRINKING

On Awakening

◆ Drink a glass (200 ml) of filtered water that has been boiled then cooled to room temperature or a little warmer. You can add lemon or honey to it for flavour. Or drink one glass of warm herb tea.

During the night the body's metabolic rate decreases. Circulation also becomes slow and wastes and poisons accumulate. The warm water or tea flushes the first residue from the system and helps the circulation to 'awaken'. It is not a shock to the internal organs in the way cold water, which can constrict the blood vessels, would be.

At Breakfast

◆ Drink fresh fruit juice as its sugar content gives you an energy boost. You can follow this with a cup of herbal or black tea or coffee.

Mid Morning

◆ Choose your favourite herbal tea and drink it throughout the morning. Generally avoid chamomile at this time though, as it may make you too relaxed and drowsy! You can make the tea in a glass plunger, stand it on your desk and keep topping it up with boiling water as herbal teas can be used more than once. These teas can be drunk hot or lukewarm but if you prefer a cooler drink, place the tea in the fridge or add ice-blocks to it.

Lunch

❖ DRINK fresh fruit or vegetable juice or soup. Then, if so desired, a cup of herbal tea, tea or coffee.

Afternoon

❖ WATER or herbal tea throughout the afternoon.

Evening

❖ BEFORE dinner if you want an alcoholic aperitif, choose one that will stimulate the digestive enzymes, such as Campari and soda or gin and tonic.

During dinner select a high quality wine. It is better to pay more for a good wine and drink less than to drink cheap wines regularly, as cheaper wines usually contain preservatives and are more detrimental to our health.

Also, if necessary drink one to two glasses of water. Ideally, water should not be drunk while eating as it will

dilute enzymes and so food will take longer to break down. Instead it is preferable to drink water 30 minutes before or after a meal.

At least ten to fifteen minutes

after dinner drink a herb tea. Mint or chamomile are ideal as they will assist the digestion of fats, calm the stomach and bowel and generally give a feeling of comfort to the system.

If you drink coffee at night make sure that it is decaffeinated so that you can still sleep well. Coffee should only be drunk in the evening if you need the stimulation of caffeine when you are going out partying and dancing or if you are studying late into the night.

Some Tips

❖ ALWAYS keep a bottle of still mineral water with you if you are not near a source of filtered water. This is an ideal way to keep up your fluid intake.

In the winter months, make a hot thermos of herbal tea or soup that you can drink during the day.

If you are recovering from drinking too much alcohol it will help to drink as much water as possible. Alternatively, make a large pot of herbal tea and keep it beside your bed then drink it throughout the night, even if it grows cool.

Offer your guests, either in business or socially, the choice of herbal tea, coffee or tea. You may be surprised at the number of people who will welcome a herbal drink. Also, keep a pot of herbal tea on the board room table during meetings along with tea and coffee. It will make a welcome change and may assist concentration.

If you do drink coffee or alcohol, balance their effects by following them with a cup of herbal tea. We can have the best of both worlds – taste, pleasure and health!

THE STRONG BREWS

Tannin

◆ MOST people are aware that black tea contains tannin, but it is also found in many medicinal herbs. Tannins are contained in the leaves and bark of some plants and herbalists use this tannin to treat certain disorders.

Through the ages tannin has been used to tan animal hides. It tightens the cell membrane, making it useful not only in the production of leather but also as the astringent component in skin toners and cosmetics.

Black tea, with its high tannin content, can actually tan the stomach if it is drunk in large quantities over a long time. This impairs the production of the digestive juices, especially inhibiting sucrose – an enzyme that is important in assisting glucose absorption. So, if you drink several cups of black tea per day you may experience poor digestion. Tannin can also interfere with iron absorption, leading to anaemia. It can often cause constipation and large doses will eventually stain your teeth.

Black tea grown in China contains approximately 7 per cent of tannin; Indian tea, 8 per cent; and oolong tea has approximately 20 per cent. The average cup of black tea that you will brew at home consists of about two grams of tannin.

It was once thought that heavy tea drinkers were more prone to contracting cancer of the oesophagus. Researchers now believe, however, that it is the extremely hot or boiling water used in the tea that may damage the lining of the throat and oesophagus, possibly causing cancer. There is also some evidence to suggest that the English who add milk to their tea, bind the tannins and so have a much lower incident of oesophageal obstruction than do the Dutch who generally drink large quantities of tea without milk.

On a herbal note, the active constituent of the medicinal plant oak bark (*Quercus robur* or *petraea*) is almost 100 per cent tannin. This tannin is well tolerated by the skin so oak bark is a wondrous plant to use externally for treating weeping eczema, varicose veins, inflammatory eye conditions and haemorrhoids.

Boil one to two tablespoons of chopped oak bark for fifteen minutes in half a litre of water. Then strain this liquid, let it cool and use it undiluted. This quantity will be sufficient for the whole day but make a new decoction each day. Saturate compresses in the tea and wring them out before applying. For weeping eczema and leg ulcers this is one of the most effective treatments and often need only be used for a few days. When the ulcer or lesions become clean, apply calendula and chamomile ointment.

Green tea contains hydrolysable tannin. It has been found to possess considerable amounts of anti-oxidants, so researchers are investigating this tea for use in preventing cancer. The incidence of lung cancer in Japan is relatively low despite the very large number of smokers.

This has been attributed to the consumption of green tea that, unlike the black tea drunk in the West, has this anti-oxidant activity.

Research into the therapeutic substances in green tea continues and in the next decade we will know even more about its medicinal uses. As for tannin in black tea, moderate consumption is the key. If you drink more than two to three cups a day you should consider changing to herbal teas as your digestive system will probably be suffering.

Caffeine

❖ CAFFEINE is the highly stimulating, active substance in black tea and coffee, some soft drinks, chocolate and some pharmaceutical drugs. It is not contained in herbal tea (except in the herb kola).

There has been much confusion over caffeine and its effects. Researchers now believe that in small amounts it has no major physical or mental side effects. If it is consumed in large amounts however, it can cause considerable problems, especially for some people who have mild or serious health disorders.

When your daily consumption of caffeine is over 350 mg (which is equivalent to four medium strength cups of coffee or eight cups of tea), you will become dependent on this substance. Consuming over 650 mg of caffeine a day can be a great risk to your health. It can increase your rate of breathing; raise your blood pressure; increase your rate of digestion; and increase the secretion of acids into the stomach. High doses of caffeine will also slow down the passage of wastes through the small intestine. However, it speeds up passage through the large intestine, leading to digestive disorders and possible diarrhoea.

Caffeine reduces the body's absorption of specific nutrients, especially iron. It increases urination by 30 per cent for up to three hours after ingestion, which can lead to excretion of calcium, magnesium and sodium. Also, as we all know, it causes chronic insomnia when consumed about an hour before going to bed. Large intakes of caffeine can cause an irregular heartbeat and you may find that your cholesterol levels can be significantly higher than they should be.

If these symptoms sound overwhelming, remember that it is surprising how much 'hidden' caffeine we consume. We can quickly eat or drink well over the recommended maximum of 350 mg of caffeine and risk suffering any of the symptoms listed above.

Although black tea contains about half as much caffeine as coffee, it also contains active substances called theophylline and theobromine. These act in a similar but milder way than caffeine.

After tea, carbonated soft drinks are rated the third highest sources of caffeine.

From the table overleaf you can quickly work out how much caffeine you really do consume per day (and this does not include any chocolate or hot cocoa drinks).

Pregnant women who have a dependency above 650 mg of caffeine per day should be aware that this puts the health of their unborn child seriously at risk. It can interfere with the duplications of DNA and cause mutations,

Caffeine content of standard drinks

Average cup coffee	80 mg
Strong cup of coffee	120 mg
Average cup tea	40 mg
Average can or bottle of soft drink	40 mg

or error, in cell reproduction. A very high caffeine intake by the mother can lead to a low birth weight. Also, children can be born with a caffeine dependency if their mothers continue to ingest large amounts of caffeine while pregnant.

Pregnant women should limit their caffeine intake to a maximum of one to two cups of coffee or one to two glasses of carbonated drinks per day.

Research on the effect of caffeine on post-menopausal women shows that if their daily consumption of caffeine is equal to or greater than the amount contained in two to three cups of coffee, they may risk accelerated bone loss from the spine. Women whose calcium intake is below the recommended daily allowance of 800 mg could suffer this bone loss throughout their whole body.

We must be aware of the consequences of drinking or eating too much caffeine. One to two cups of coffee and one to two cups of tea would be more than enough each day. Try drinking herbal teas instead and gradually cut down your caffeine intake.

If you suffer from peptic and duodenal ulcers, irritable bowel, colitis, eczema, arthritis, anxiety, high blood pressure and are experiencing high levels of stress, you should abstain from coffee and other caffeine drinks and foods completely.

On the positive side, and for those who do not suffer health problems, caffeine can keep you alert while you are studying or during long-distance driving. It helps to get us going in the morning (not on an empty stomach), and is good as an occasional pick-me-up through the day.

Alcohol

❖ WHEN you drink alcohol in moderation, and if you choose a good quality drink that is appropriate for your state of health, it can be a great way to help you relax. In excess however, alcohol is a poison with severe effects on the liver, brain cells and the nervous system.

More than a few glasses of alcohol can be extremely dehydrating, and you should drink water in between glasses of wine. Unfortunately, many preservatives, additives and ferments are included in wine and it is often these substances that cause headaches, dry and irritated skin and a bloated feeling. The preservatives also often trigger histamine reactions for those who suffer sinus problems.

❖

'Australia has the distinction of having
the hightest rate of alcohol
related brain damage in the world.'

ROSEMARY STANTON
Eating for Health

❖

On the more positive side, studies are being carried out on the polyphenolic compounds of red wine. These substances have been found to be similar to the main components of the hawthorn berry and may protect you against coronary heart disease.

If you suffer from the effects of yeast avoid wine and beer, even though they have a lower alcohol content than distilled spirits. Otherwise you may experience poor digestion, skin irritation and upper respiratory tract allergies.

Brewed drinks such as beer, ale and stout go through a number of fermentation processes and are usually made from cereals. If you are allergic to a particular grain it is wise to avoid the alcoholic drink that is made from that grain. Also, malt, which is made from barley, is a large component of these beverages and sufferers of skin allergies will react to it badly.

Some people find that purer alcoholic drinks such as vodka are less aggravating to their health. I suggest that you drink gin and tonic or vodka and tonic in moderation if you have an allergic reaction to wine or beer.

If you want to drink alcohol socially, follow these guidelines and you will feel much better the next day.

❖ Line the stomach first or eat while you are drinking, unless you choose a mild aperitif such as Campari and soda.

❖ Drink good quality wines as they have the lowest amount of additives and preservatives.

❖ Red wine is better for an acid stomach than white wine or champagne.

❖ Avoid beer and highly fermented spirits if you suffer from yeast allergies, a bloated stomach or indigestion.

❖ Drink a glass of water for every glass of wine or spirit to dilute the effect. Unfortunately this does not apply to beer as water and beer will aggravate your stomach.

❖ Drink in moderation only and be prepared to say no to offers of further rounds from heavy drinking friends. Remember that you will pay the price for excessive drinking the next day and in the long term.

If you suffer an acid stomach, peptic ulcer or have a history of hepatitis or liver weakness, avoid alcohol altogether.

CONCLUSION

*J*UST as our ancestors have done for hundreds of years, we now use herbs for their fresh and enticing tastes and for the benefits that they can bring us. Berries, leaves, flowers and roots are the delicious and healthy ingredients of herbal tea. Select them according to your individual tastes and needs; the variety is enormous.

It may take you some time to change your old drinking habits but as you do so you will be rewarded with increased energy and a healthier state of mind. Start with a herbal tea that you like then experiment with others. I believe that as we drink these teas, our taste buds change and we begin to look forward to them as we might also look forward to a cappuccino or a cup of black tea. Then gradually we will no longer crave sweet, carbonated drinks or large amounts of alcohol or coffee.

I am optimistic that in the future further research will be carried out on the beneficial effects of plants, complementing the traditional knowledge. More and more people will turn to medicinal herbs and natural treatments to maintain or improve their health. The coming of the year 2000 should signal an awareness in everyone that our bodies and our environment must be cleaner, purer and healthier.

I drink to your good health!